THE MOON IS ALMOST FULL

THE MOON IS ALMOST FULL

Chana Bloch

Autumn House Press

PITTSBURGH

"Autumn House Press" and "Autumn House" are registered trademarks owned by
Autumn House Press, a nonprofit corporation whose mission is the publication
and promotion of poetry and other fine literature.

 Autumn House Press receives state arts
funding support through a grant from
the Pennsylvania Council on the Arts,
a state agency funded by the Commonwealth of Pennsylvania, and the
National Endowment for the Arts, a federal agency.

ISBN: 978-1-938769-20-7
Library of Congress Control Number: 2017936835

All Autumn House books are printed on acid-free paper and meet the international
standards for permanent books intended for purchase by libraries.

for my dear family
and my family of friends
and for my grandchildren

Also by Chana Bloch

POETRY

Swimming in the Rain
Blood Honey
Mrs. Dumpty
The Past Keeps Changing
The Secrets of the Tribe

TRANSLATION

Yehuda Amichai, *Open Closed Open* (with Chana Kronfeld)
Yehuda Amichai, *The Selected Poetry* (with Stephen Mitchell)
Dahlia Ravikovitch, *Hovering at a Low Altitude: The Collected Poetry*
   (with Chana Kronfeld)
Dahlia Ravikovitch, *The Window: New and Selected Poems*
   (with Ariel Bloch)
Dahlia Ravikovitch, *A Dress of Fire*
The Song of Songs (with Ariel Bloch)

SCHOLARSHIP

Spelling the Word: George Herbert and the Bible

Contents

Yom Asal, Yom Basal   1

I

Three Wishes   5
Bucket List   6
Taking the Waters   7
Rosh Hashana in the Field   8
Doing Time   9
Inside Out   10
Sunday at the Vivarium   11
A Quid for a Quo   12
Dying for Dummies   13
Provisions   14
Babel   15
Divide   16
The Mind-Body Problem   17
My Day's Last Race   18
Prayer   19
Shadowland   20

II

Memento Mori   23
The Face of Death   24
Buying Time   25
Plan B   26
At the Intersection   27

Pentimento   28

He Lived for Beauty   29

The Persistence of Memory   30

Key   31

Their Kind of Talk   33

Under the Rug   34

Safeway 24/7   35

The Feast   36

The Great Samovar   37

Sisters   38

Shipwreck   39

Settling the Account   40

Cancer Ward   41

III

Song   45

Instructions for the Bridegroom   46

Eros   47

Desire   48

Unimaginable   49

Regarding the Pain of Others   50

Her Mourning   51

Case Closed   52

Dominion Blues   53

Bequest   54

The Ephemerals   55

Dear Future,   56

Death Row   57

Deadlines   58

The Will   60

Memorizing the City   62
Moon over Menlo Place   63

Acknowledgments   67
About the Author   69

THE MOON IS ALMOST FULL

Yom Asal, Yom Basal

One day honey, one day onion.
                    —Arabic saying

In every maybe the fear of yes.
In every promise a shattered glass.

For every portion a cutting edge.
For every rift a slippery bridge.

In every hope some pickling salt.
In every bungle a touch of guilt.

Unto every plan God's ringing laughter.
Unto every death a morning after.

I

And now in age I bud again,
After so many deaths I live and write;
   I once more smell the dew and rain,
And relish versing.

—*George Herbert,*
"The Flower"

Three Wishes

The first is always foolish, the second
a foolish attempt to undo it.
But it was you

who made those wishes, you
with your regrettable failure
to see around corners.

What are you saving the third wish for?

You've lived on roots, slept on straw,
looked down a well so deep
you couldn't see bottom.

The horizon is just beginning
to tighten its wire
around you—

That's no cloth of gold,
just the setting sun
gilding the windows.

Bucket List

We got ourselves all the way to Corfu
to see "the most beautiful sunset in Europe."
There we sat and waited, shivering under winter skies.
A silver line on the horizon.
After a while, another. "Travel narrows the mind,"
one of us joked. I forget which of us laughed.
Cross off China. Cross off the steamy rain forest
in Costa Rica, the three-museum days that almost
did us in. This evening, in my regal wine-dark robe,
I receive the sunset at my kitchen window.
Forget the future. The past is a continent
barely mapped, and deep enough,
down to the earth's hot core.

Taking the Waters

Nobody here looks good
in a bathing suit.
Every body has a story,

ladies with epic thighs
and creaky joints,
gents with wobbly knees,

the halt and the lame
strapping weights at the ankle,
weights at the waist.

The bodies take to the water
where every hurt is healed
in the blessèd *Eau de chlorine.*

Arms and legs slog away
in the dark, underwater,
while heads converse.

My body takes me to the deep end
where the sun presides, summer
flooding the high windows.

I close my eyes.
I'm racing from dock to raft,
faster than all the boys.

Rosh Hashana in the Field

Year 5746 of Creation, I sat between my sons,
in a stuffy room, Prayer Book in hand.
This is the birthday of the world!
the cantor incanted.
A blast of the ram's horn made it official.

On Rosh Hashana it is inscribed,
and on Yom Kippur it is sealed:
Who shall live and who shall die.
But prayer and repentance
avert the severe decree.

"You believe in that stuff?" the little one whispered
a little too loud: "I believe in the Big Bang."
The older one poked my side:
"Another hauntingly beautiful melody."

Thirty years later, *Hineni*, here I am
among the beasts of the field
ages before the birth of words.
God is busy today with the penitents.
I have the earth and the fullness thereof
all to myself. *Blessed be.*

A sparrow lands on a springy stalk,
rides it fluently to the ground.
The deer come up close and present their ears.

Doing Time

Day goes on collecting
grains of fatigue
one o'clock
two o'clock
that lodge in the tissue,
sleeper cells
three o'clock
four
growing secretly.
I hardly notice when day
five o'clock
six o'clock
slips into dark.
At first I hardly noticed
seven o'clock
eight
the lump. The first
raindrops on the pavement
nine o'clock
ten o'clock
are a casual spatter. All at once
eleven o'clock
twelve—
the sidewalk is slick.

Inside Out

It is either serious or it isn't.
The indeterminate mass, 14.8 cm long,
is either a cyst or a tumor.
If a tumor, either benign or malignant.
If malignant, either slow-growing,
or aggressive, in which case
they may contain it. If not,
no one else will recall
this unseasonable day of waiting
as you did, from the inside out
—the way the heat of your mind
dropped a few degrees
and grew very quiet. The sediment
settled. Then you consulted
the uncommon clarity of the sky.
A mild translucent blue: a sign,
perhaps. The leaves held still
in the almost imperceptible breeze,
though at the tips of the branches
the first buds of spring
were so closefisted
you couldn't be sure
whether you saw them, or not.

Sunday at the Vivarium

Lacewing, Swallowtail, Morpho
—to them I am landscape.
One alights on my finger
and beats its wings.
A mating dance? "No," says the docent.
"It shivers like that when it's cold."

"The butterfly dines on nectar of lily
but looks to urine and dung
for its daily salt. Life,"
says the docent, "eats what it eats.
What it wants is more life."

Like the cells multiplying inside me,
the cells with an appetite
for the body's sugars,
the ones that light up on the scan.
In the humid rain forest atrium
I feel a chill.

"I'm fine." A shivery song
you've heard me sing.
When you see me flutter and flit around,
don't be fooled,
I'm just trying to stay warm.

A Quid for a Quo

That musty sickroom smelling of cancer.

"My mother is dying," Sonya told me
on the way home from school.
"Dying," she said, and broke into a run.

"So unfair! God, take my grandma instead,"
I wrote in my diary
—a human sacrifice

to the Lord of the Flaring Nostrils
who speaks Leviathan,
a language with twenty words for *sacrifice*.

All that year I kept watch on God
and on Grandma, gathering dust
at the Daughters of Jacob Old Age Home

where we'd find her each Friday
troubled by kidney stones and time,
mumbling "God will provide."

Dying for Dummies

I used to study the bigger kids
—they'd show-and-tell me
how to wiggle my hips,
how to razz the boys.

Now I'm watching my cohort
master the skills at each grade
of incapacity
and get promoted to the next.

To the oldest I'm a novice.
"These seventy-five-year-olds,
they think they know everything,"
says Cousin Leo. He's ninety.

Who thinks, Leo? Who knows?

We're too busy reading *Gratitude*
and *Being Mortal*,
passing around the revised edition
of *Dying for Dummies*,

still trying to get it right.
And the young study us.

Provisions

In memory of Jane Cooper

"What's left for me to write?"
I asked the aging poet. I was thirty,
she was amused.

"Life will provide," she answered,
Delphic, though her tone
was maternal.

A woman weathered and tempered
and well-provisioned for the life
that mauled her hands.

I thought she meant the monster
crouched in the labyrinth—Life
that eats us alive.

But it was the ball of twine,
the endless thread,
the poem.

Babel

for Benjamin and Jonathan

They used to conspire in a brother-tongue
no one else could parse.
They were its sole native speakers,
these sons I raised
on the habit of food and talk.

Who are these children
with their beards and glasses,
two Men of Babel jabbering away,
each in his own tongue?

When I was twelve, I begged my mother,
"Don't get twin beds," imagining
a nightstand foursquare and mute as a gravestone,
the two of them buried on either side.

Two sons in the keep of my kitchen:
the slightest pause and I rush to translate.
Let them speak one language again
the way they used to.
This is still my house.

Divide

"That photo you sent,
the one of you on Fisherman's Wharf
with a white cockatoo on your shoulder
—why did you send it? what does it mean?
Everything has a meaning."

"Except when it doesn't," you answer back,
laughing.

Then come the questions a mother
can't ask a son.
An Index of Forbidden Topics.
"I have something to say, but you won't like it."
"Then don't say it."

The shortest distance between two people
is still a distance
in the hill country where we live.
No way to measure the pause from "How are you?"
to "Fine, I'm fine."

Like a charged synapse,
the crackle of silence between us
could be the divide
that binds.

The Mind-Body Problem

Those were the days, my friend,
when we were a two-in-one.
Just summon Mind
and Body was right on the spot,

thinking what Mind would feel.
Ergo: I was. We was. We were
an item, one flesh, a marriage
perfused with mind.

"Descartes, you had it all wrong,"
we crowed with a single voice.
Oh the living was easy,
when we were a two-in-one.

Now we're divorced and quartered
in the same ruined house.
I wash its hands and face;
it spends my time.

Evenings I manage to catch a break.
When my body goes to bed,
I get to stay up half the night
and think.

My Day's Last Race

Ecclesiastes 9:11

"I'm not betting against you," says the doctor
in his New Jersey accent, Hawaiian shirt.
"I'm not betting for you, either.
It's even money."

He swipes at the keyboard once, twice,
and he's out the door,
strutting the Halls of Oncology.

Let him go. This is my day's last race.
Let's assume we're in luck.
Let's assume time and chance are with us.

Let's keep eating the bread
of assumption, drinking
the sugared wine.

Prayer

There being no one to pray to
we pray to Life
which gets larger and larger
the smaller we get.

We stand up straight
as we were taught
but the vertebrae settle.

We're too old to pray
Let me not die.
Even the chairs that outlive us
won't last.

What we ask
gets quicker and quicker
the slower we get:
Let me not die
Let me not

while I'm alive.

Shadowland

Specimen cups and vials
     take my measure
          in cc's of crimson and gold,
my body's royal colors.
     Under siege I am still
          a kingdom
I tell myself,
     though here in the waiting room
          I'll say anything.
The shadow that follows me
     falls on the hillside,
          leaves a chill on the valley.
This climate I live in,
     this waiting,
          this flustering bracing
unabating gray—
     Whatever I ask, it answers:
          "Maybe."

II

I learned to speak among the pains.

—*Yehuda Amichai,*
"The Precision of Pain"

Memento Mori

"God blessed you with curly hair,"
my mother used to say
and dressed me like Shirley Temple.

On my bare scalp, Australia:
a birthmark that hid
in the thicket of my hair.

Unblessed in a downburst, I lost
my leafy summer, my lovely,
my crest, my crown.

I sleep in a flannel nightcap.
My wig sleeps in a closet,
comb and brush in a drawer.

I wake to a still life—
a clock that marks the hour
before it strikes.

No skull on my desk.
Just a face in the mirror,
unrecognizable.

The Face of Death

No one can look upon the Face of God
and live. Even Moses could not.
That nuclear fury
would have blazed him to a char.

The Face of Death has me in its sights,
blistering cold as dry ice.
I may look upon it if I dare. And I must.
O Death, thou knowest.

I refuse to turn my eyes away.
I am choosing day by day to see
even as I am seen, till the last face-to-face
when I am taken with a kiss.

Buying Time

John Muir Hospital

I pay with the very hairs of my head,
each one numbered
before it falls.

My eyebrows, lashes, the body hair
that made me a woman.
Unsexed, I'm a wizened child.

My granddaughter pets my fuzzy head.
The wall clock keeps time
up out of reach.

What does it say? *"Tick-tock,*
Grandma." I taught her that.
The clock knows the price

of the toxic *drip-drop.*
When the tubing kinks, the pump
goes *beep beep.*

Here comes the nurse, hazmat-suited,
severe. "Pay up," she says.
I give my right arm.

Plan B

I'm tethered to the hospital wall.
Nurses enter without knocking.
A cold coin listens up and down my back:
"Take a deep breath." My lungs
sigh for the stethoscope.

When no one is looking,
I'll unplug the IV pole,
steal through the marble lobby
with its potted Jurassic ferns,
and find my way back to my old green life—

At the Intersection

"I knocked on a door and it opened."

"The door was half-open?"

"No, the door was shut,
I didn't think anyone was there."

"Then why did you knock?"

"I was tired by then, it was Friday,
late afternoon. I had given up trying."

"But why did you knock?"

"Before I could speak, I heard a voice:
'Come in. Have a seat.'"

"I know that place, at the intersection
of self and door. More than once
I've walked past it."

"What are you saying?"

"More than once I've stood before it like you
but didn't dare."

Pentimento

This paint takes a while to dry.
It's your canvas, your brush, and you
can still make a change.
Why not a window over there, instead of
an unmade bed?

Now open the window
to a painter's sky, rack of cloud and all.
You could loft yourself up and away
on a puff of regret.

You've painted one failure after another
out of the picture
though traces remain, the story
behind the story.

Your hand knows only what it likes
and it tells you. But the infrared knows
how many wrong moves it took you
to make a life.

He Lived for Beauty

Color was what he required,
and women, warm or cool.
Ochre, burnt umber, cerulean:
he dipped his brush.

How he relished the final touches:
rose petals, rose nipples,
the wingtips of birds.

Even a lick of sunlight on moss,
a stem of freesia in a glass.

He's done with beauty, but not before
beauty is done with him.

The world he loved, let them have it!
—the young
with the young in their arms.

The Persistence of Memory

My ex sits beside me on a bench at Starbucks
a week before our son's wedding.
The little or nothing we manage
over coffee and muffins—
Hello, who are you, I am fine—
is sticky with complication.

I divorced the past, pasted
new memories over the used ones,
composted the roses.

Still it lives
in the twist of my mouth,
a whir in the inner ear
that comes uninvited, keeps me
off-balance.

In the safety of Starbucks
I corner myself:
Why did you stay so long?

Over the clatter of cups and spoons,
I can hear him think:
You're not done with me yet.
I'll follow you home, I'll muddle your dreams.
When you're flat on your back, so help me,
I'll find you.

Key

I make a key   to my house
for the man   I love
When I hand it   to him
my hand   pulls back
pulls me   back to a country
road   getting darker

That man   was a neighbor
I hardly knew   unthinking I
stepped into his car   into
his summer shirt
unbuttoned   the dark
hair on his arm

I have a gun   he said
to the steering wheel   I think   I stared
at his profile   his
hand on the wheel   the chain-link
watchband   flash of steel

Where   are we going   so fast
I kept   looking for a sign
my foot   kept feeling   for a brake

It gets dark   even faster
these days   the sediments   rise
when they please   they
choose the moment   not I

I hand the key to my house
to the man   I love
I think

Their Kind of Talk

That couple speaking
sign language in the park,

how they go at it—weave and
pivot, swivel and dip!

Or the way our maestro
can rouse

air and brass and string
with a wink of his baton.

Come woo me, love,
I'm in a holiday mood!

Let's count the ways
in body English.

A word that thinks twice
when the music starts

is shy as a kiss
with no hands.

Under the Rug

goes the argument you and I had
better not have.
One lick of the broom.

Not just any rug. This one's a Persian
that still holds the angry stain
of my first marriage.
Now it lies at our door.

The vegetable dyes—flush
of wild madder,
moody indigo blues—
are brighter on the underside.

A tale is woven into the carpet.
The weaver, a woman, let's say,
packed the weft, knotted the wool
and left a flaw as she was taught:

Allah alone is perfect.

Safeway 24/7

We walked out with summer
bagged and paid for:
strawberries piled in plastic coffers,
raspberries, blueberries,
shade-grown Jamaican coffee.

He has only his open hand
and his sweetly accusatory
"Bless you." We have only
to turn our heads and he's gone.

We'll be home in no time
to naked comforts. Fall asleep
to the purring of the fridge—

Who says we have to offer a cloak to every
poor soul on Solano? Remorse
is its own reward.

Cherries and plums on special today,
and black oil sunflower seeds
for our little sisters the sparrows,
who are always hungry.

The Feast

Schadenfreude is best served hot
but room temperature will do,

and chilled, it will not lose its savor.
It may be enjoyed in high-toned

privacy, or passed around the table
for boisterous second helpings.

It's the poor man's supper,
but the rich are as quick to help themselves.

As we sit down to eat our fill,
even the smallest taste

will betray
how insatiable we are.

The Great Samovar

Two chipped glasses on a tray
and a lemon, sliced.

"How about a *glezele tey*, honey?
So long as you're here, sit down,
have a bite to eat, it shouldn't be a total loss."
Even a glass of tea
may be subject to market forces.

So how's life, Auntie?
"Don't ask."

Whatever gets poured from the Great Samovar
falls straight to the bottom line.
She sees only the glint of emptiness
at the top of the glass.

Auntie, listen,
we've all got tickers ticking away
to figure down to the penny
how little we get to keep—

She blows on the hot tea and takes a sip.
"What a bill of goods they sold us, honey.
It's all a gyp."

Sisters

for Liliana

In the beginning was the breast milk, warm.
She was a mouth in search of a nipple,
an only child in the nook of Mama's arm.
Then Baby bared its gums.

Poke-poke at Mama's vacant belly:
"I'm *frustrated* at the baby."
Oh what a find for almost-three
—that word's a keeper.

In no time she's promoted to Big Sister
with all the hurts and privileges
pertaining thereunto. She can master
the entire vocabulary of pain

now that she commands
a tongue, a capable mouth.
Let milk be milk!
The big new word has teeth.

Shipwreck

The dead will tell you:
There is always one who abandons
a sinking ship,
the one you'd least expect.

The one who says, with drama at the door,
"I love you like a sister." *Love! Love!*
Words, words
that plummet at a touch.

No use trying to fathom
froth on a wake,
fairweather songs in a storm.

The ship is going, going under,
and with a "Bye-bye, I'll pray for you!"
she's gone.

Settling the Account

"You can afford to be generous," she'd say
with that cost-accounting of hers
that never failed to leave me
impoverished.

For years I let her.
Now I've been scrapping
people and props, furniture, crockery,
patching up fissures of the heart.
I'm feeding regrets
to the teeth of the garbage disposal.
Let it grind away with a joyful noise.

One thing more: I can be generous
with a vengeance,
do her a good turn without
her knowing. And this time I won't
keep my motives secret
from myself.

I'm repairing the past because finally,
finally I can afford to.

Cancer Ward

A joy so acute it startles me.

Here, on this mountain pass
where dangers multiply,

fates with an appetite—

a clearing of bright
cold-bladed air.

Even here, on this corridor,
this slippery-when-wet,

a clarity.

As if joy required
only joys to feed it.

III

and here I am fighting this
ferocious insane vindictive virus day and
night   day and night   and for what?   for only
one thing   this life   this life

> —*Grace Paley,*
> *"This Life"*

Song

for Benjamin and Trang

Their book of poems
is bound in green.
Treetop green, like
the new spring leaves
that sweeten
the air we breathe.

And the lovers,
bridegroom and bride,
are binding themselves
one to the other
in a love that livens
the air they breathe.

I speak for the mothers
who cry at weddings.
I speak for the lovers,
husband and wife.
I speak for the leaves.

Instructions for the Bridegroom

Under the canopy, break a glass
to remember the Romans

demolished that Temple of yours.
Mazel tov! But don't get too happy.

Never forget
you were put on earth to gather joy

with melancholy hands.
Now you may kiss the bride,

your rose of Sharon, your darling
among the shards.

Eros

The way one touch
invites another
till it takes just a breath,
a shudder,
the tip of the tongue.

Or the way a word,
a blurt of language
on the page,
may beget a poem.

It needs the dark to grow.
Give it time and enough
of your darkness.
You already have within you
more than enough.

Desire

Saturday night extravaganzas,
quilts and pillows on the living room floor,
the slinky red nightgown,
a Shostakovich CD,
slices of mango and pear laid out on a plate,
a few puffs of weed—
Enough? No, it's just the prologue to wanting more.

Now I live for the least of my desires
like Ivan Ilyich, who rejoiced
sixteen pages before his death
when his servant Gerasim lifted his aching legs
and held them on his shoulders all night long
to ease the pain.

Unimaginable

1

To my German boyfriend I sent
grandiloquent poems when I was twenty
about "the blood of history" that kept us apart.
He argued back on sheer blue airmail paper:
"You and I can change the past."

He was wrong,
but not as wrong as I was.

2

Impossible to conjure a future
I didn't choose.

A life in which these sons of mine
would not appear.

 "You can't change just one variable,"
they insist, quick to defend

their right to a life.
They can't imagine their not being.

As they can't imagine my not being.
As I can't imagine my not—

Regarding the Pain of Others

for Amira Hass and Idith Zertal

As Amira's mother was deported to Bergen-Belsen, the local women passed by with their shopping baskets: "They watched us taken away with a curious indifference. Or was it an indifferent curiosity?"

The wife of the Nazi schoolteacher in Lanzmann's *Shoah*: "It was frightful! Depressing. Day after day, the same spectacle! You can't force a whole village to watch such distress. It gets on your nerves."

Or the women lined up at the ditch in Ponary, waiting to be shot, who covered their naked bodies, breast and crotch, with their hands. Someone recorded their humiliation. Printed and framed the photo. Hung it on a museum wall, so the women and what they were desperate to hide could be seen.

Her Mourning

Whenever we mention closure,
the latest advance in grief hygiene,

she laughs. Then out come the hankies:
"I'm grieving as fast as I can."

When he lay dying we told her,
"Keep talking to him,

he'll hear you.
Hearing is the last sense to go."

Now she gives us the look.
She's hopeless, that woman!

So she keeps talking, talking,
and he keeps on being dead.

Case Closed

The forty-three endless battering C major chords at the absolute end
of the Fifth Symphony,
Beethoven's unsurpassed finalissimo:

Causa finita est!

Then a gust of silence

clears the air.

You must ignore the coughing,
the shuffling shoes,
to attend to its properties.

You must listen closely to hear
the timbre of silence
which has its own music

and like a poem—or a death—
may have
something unsettling to propose.

Dominion Blues

There's hope for a tree, when you cut it down,
The Bible says, when you cut it down,
At the scent of water it sprouts from the ground.

It ain't necessarily so, we said.
We know how to kill a tree till it's dead.
We know how to kill things good and dead.

On Easter Island they cut down the trees,
Called as they cut down the last of the trees:
Dominion is ours! We do as we please.

Some people say: They did themselves in.
People are saying we'll do ourselves in.
But where does it say that dominion's a sin?

Dominion's an art, like anything else.
Dominion is ours, like everything else.
The earth is ours; we'll do as we please.

Bequest

The Golden Record aboard Voyager, 1977

We wanted to make a good impression. Maybe even to launch a conversation.

Bonjour in fifty-five languages—some, like Sumerian and Akkadian, long dead.

Bach, Beethoven, Chuck Berry, the *tap-tap* of Morse code, birdsong and whale song.

The silhouette of a naked man and woman made the final cut, but no nude photographs. Taxpayers were adamant. Not even a naked baby.

And no photos of war or nuclear explosions. They might get ideas.

A billion years from now, when the earth is a charred cinder, our Voyager may land on some friendly galactic shore. And with it, the Golden Record, our calling card.

To Whom It May Concern: We just wanted to drop by and say, *Hello, how are you? We were fine.*

The Ephemerals

after Andy Goldsworthy's
Rivers and Tides

That an artist can get blood from a stone!
He grinds river rocks to a powder,
tosses handfuls into the sky
and a creature of dust rears up, a red ephemeral
braced with iron, like us.

Now he's at work before dawn.
His frozen fingers weld icicles into crescents,
fuse them to the flanks of a stone.
The rising sun lights them incandescent
till they smolder and fall away.

Now he's stitching a rope of hazel leaves
with stalks of dry grass,
his gift to a rock pool. Watch, watch
as the water unwinds it,
sends it snaking downriver to death.

He pushes each work to the verge of collapse
where it is most acutely itself,
just before the elements
are set free as energy:

green lightning skittering away
when the wind snags the current,
icicles thawed by the sun,
the blood cloud of life
that rains itself out in drops of glowing dust.

Dear Future,

my own, my only, it is you I conjure
as I take in the mail and the paper,
impatient to open and unfold.
Your low clouds threaten the morning.

Are you listening?
All that living of mine must have
some use. I'm not greedy,
just curious to know
the uses you will make of me.

Your Honor, I have been innocent
after my fashion. May it please the Court
to commute my sentence
to life without parole—

I section the grapefruit,
spoon a little honey into the cup,
hope a little hope,
and here you are already,
waiting to tell me:

"All that hoping—
I could have told you."

Death Row

I envy Cleopatra, Queen of Egypt:
she took the time to study
One Hundred Easy Ways to Die.
Exultant in crown and robe, she chose
the asp, that *pretty worm of the Nile,*
swooned at its potent kiss.

Anne Boleyn prayed to be spared
all the way to the scaffold. Her luck
was the master swordsman from Calais,
his whetted blade,
the way he slipped behind her,
took her by surprise.

Not like the prisoner on death row
who is given his date.
His solitary countdown begins
under the lizard eye of the camera
—prevented from suicide, as the law requires,
to be delivered up safely unto death.

Just not like my dear father,
deranged in lung and limb,
slamming his arm against the mattress
"to hurt the pain." If only he'd asked
I would have brought what was needed,
crushed in his applesauce.

Deadlines

1865

Thousands of Union soldiers were confined in Andersonville
in a stockade of rough-hewn logs. Around its inside perimeter
was a rail they called the "dead line." Any prisoner who dared
to "touch, fall upon, pass over, under, or across the dead line"
was shot by the guards on sight.

1960

How I hated the pounding of dread under pressure,
the typewriter *clickety-clacking* away after midnight,
haze of NoDoz and glop of Wite-Out,
the deadline strung tight from late to later.
How I loved it.

2016

To have lived all my life
with that deadrail
inside the very walls,
invisible—

What I need to do, I need to do
quickly, before it's too late:

last will last wishes
casket or ashes. Decide!

And then to finish the assignment,
pounding the keyboard
in a fury of words
as that rail rushes at me,

instant, electric.

The Will

Let the university send a couple of students
to cart off the Russian novels
I was always meaning to read.
Let the world take note
how long I intended to live.

My plans and projects I hereby bequeath to the air
of which they were conceived.
Let others go on confecting without
benefit of fact; let them try to map
an overland route to Mars.

Let my heirs distribute, howsoever they wish,
my earrings, angers, scratchy old vinyls,
the Baskin etching of a wild boar
bristling like a hairbrush jammed in a drawer,
the jumbo umbrella that stood guard at the door
all through the drought.

To my husband and sons I leave our house
and the resident fauna:
bees who turn nectar into solvent in the walls,
mice in the rafters who dine on fiberglass,
deer who graze on our city street
between parked cars.

Let the doctors pack up my heart
and keep it humming for the right customer.
Let it go on accruing interest
in some other body.

All my loved ones I leave
to this life, which will change them
just as it changes you. And you—if you can use it,
I leave you this poem.

Memorizing the City

Wild poppies under the BART tracks,
flashes of light and shade
strobing the bikers' lane.

Every green of the grass. The trees.
Even the workaday traffic lights,
emerald or jade.

The volcanic rock outcroppings,
ancient stone gods
that save our houses from earthquake.

And the grounds of Sunset View:
a backhoe always rearing,
roughing out a new grave.

I catch myself trying to learn it by heart
so I won't forget.
The way I took in the Cinque Terre

or the Kalalau Trail,
each *Look! Look!* the click of an eye:
I won't be back.

Moon over Menlo Place

for Dave

The moon is almost full
or just past fullness.
Never mind. Up there in the milky spill
it's a good enough moon
for the likes of us,

though God knows we'd prefer
the gold-spangled moons of Jupiter,
Galileo's moons,
mantled in oceans and ice and inconceivable life,

the four with their storied names,
Io, Europa, Ganymede, Callisto,
lovers of Jove the Insatiable, ravished
and held in his gravitational pull.

What a glory to know the sun
doesn't rise or set for us!

The moon over Menlo Place,
that old lovers' moon, our one and only—
let's take it, love,
moon dust and all.

Acknowledgments

My thanks to the editors of the following journals, where these poems first appeared (some in earlier versions or with different titles):

Catamaran: Moon over Menlo Place

The Cortland Review: Three Wishes

Field: Yom Asal, Yom Basal; Cancer Ward

Grey: The Persistence of Memory, Key

Literary Imagination: Shadowland

The Manhattan Review: Rosh Hashana in the Field, The Great
    Samovar, Instructions for the Bridegroom

The New Yorker: Memento Mori, *Dying for Dummies*

Poem International Review: Dominion Blues

Poet Lore: Eros, Death Row, The Will

Prairie Schooner: Under the Rug

The Progressive: Regarding the Pain of Others

Southern Poetry Review: Doing Time, At the Intersection, He
    Lived for Beauty, The Feast

Spillway: My Last Day's Race, Pentimento

Talking Writing: A Quid for a Quo, Bequest

Tikkun: Babel, Safeway 24/7

Zeek: Their Kind of Talk

"Inside Out" is reprinted, with revisions, from *Swimming in the
    Rain: New and Selected Poems, 1980-2015* (Autumn House Press).

Finally, profound gratitude to my dear family and friends, for wisdom and sustenance. To Dave Sutter, my husband, who has made each day possible.

My thanks to Chiquita Babb for her elegant book design and imaginative cover, and to Angus Macpherson for his dazzling painting.

And most especially to my editor at Autumn House, Christine Stroud, who read the manuscript with extraordinary attention to detail and offered many valuable suggestions.

And to my poetry friends, for their demanding criticism, with special thanks to those who critiqued the final version: Benjamin Bloch, Barry and Lorrie Goldensohn, Ellen Bass, Andrea Hollander, and (always my first and last), Chana Kronfeld.

About the Author

CHANA BLOCH (1940—2017), the author of award-winning books of poetry, translation, and scholarship, was Professor Emerita of English at Mills College, where she taught for over thirty years and directed the Creative Writing Program. From 2007-2012 she served as the first poetry editor of *Persimmon Tree*, an online journal of the arts by women over sixty.

Her poetry has appeared in *Atlantic Monthly, Field, The Nation, The New Yorker, Poet Lore, The Iowa Review, Poetry, Threepenny Review,* and many other journals. It has been reprinted in *The Addison Street Anthology, The Autumn House Anthology of Contemporary American Poetry, Best American Poetry, Chapter and Verse, Don't Leave Hungry, The Extraordinary Tide, The Face of Poetry, Jewish in America, Living in the Land of Limbo, The Place That Inhabits Us, Pushcart Prize* VI and XXIX, *When She Named Fire,* and elsewhere.

In addition to her poetry collections, *The Secrets of the Tribe, The Past Keeps Changing, Mrs. Dumpty, Blood Honey,* and *Swimming in the Rain,* Bloch co-translated the biblical *Song of Songs, The Selected Poetry of Yehuda Amichai* and his *Open Closed Open,* and *Hovering at a Low Altitude: The Collected Poetry of Dahlia Ravikovitch.* She was also the author of a scholarly study, *Spelling the Word: George Herbert and the Bible.* Her poems and translations have been set to music, notably *Chana's Story,* a song cycle by David Del Tredici, and *The Song of Songs,* a cantata by the late Jorge Liderman.

Her book awards include the Poetry Society of America's Alice Fay Di Castagnola Award, the Felix Pollak Prize in Poetry, and the PEN Award for Poetry in Translation (with Chana Kronfeld). Other honors include the Meringoff Poetry Award, two fellowships from the National Endowment for the Arts, the Writers Exchange Award of Poets & Writers, two Pushcart Prizes, and the Discovery Award of the 92nd Street Y Poetry Center.

A native New Yorker, Bloch lived in Berkeley since 1967. She was married to Dave Sutter and had two grown sons, Benjamin and Jonathan, from her marriage to Ariel Bloch.

Audio and video clips of readings may be found on her website, www.chanabloch.com, and on *Voetica: Poetry Spoken*.

DESIGN AND PRODUCTION

Text and cover design: Chiquita Babb

Cover illustration: Angus Macpherson, "Giant Moon," 34" x 28", acrylic on canvas. Albuquerque painter known for his billowing clouds and trees reaching for the heavens represented at Sumner & Dene Gallery, www.sumnerdene.com.

Author photograph: Lonny Shavelson, photowords.com

The interior text of this book was typeset in Mrs Eaves; display elements were set in AT Sackers Roman. Mrs Eaves, a serif typeface designed by Zuzana Licko in 1996, is based on Baskerville, a font designed by John Baskerville in Birmingham, England, in the 1750s. The typeface is named after Sarah Eaves, Baskerville's wife.

This book was printed by McNaughton & Gunn on 55 lb. Glatfelter Natural.